This Planner Belongs to

LOVEOFLINK PUBLISHERS

Want a free printable?!

Email us at:
loveoflink@gmail.com

Title the email 'MLM Planner' and let us know you bought one of our planners.

Find us on Instagram
@OliviaLanaeBooks

My Weekly Planner

TOP GOALS	MONDAY	TUESDAY	WEDNESDAY
☐			
☐			
☐			
☐			
☐			
☐			

TO DO:

☐
☐
☐
☐
☐
☐
☐
☐
☐
☐

BILLS TO PAY

	$
	$
	$
	$
	$

APPOINTMENTS//CALLS

HABIT TRACKER

	M	T	W	T	F	S	S
	☐	☐	☐	☐	☐	☐	☐
	☐	☐	☐	☐	☐	☐	☐
	☐	☐	☐	☐	☐	☐	☐
	☐	☐	☐	☐	☐	☐	☐
	☐	☐	☐	☐	☐	☐	☐
	☐	☐	☐	☐	☐	☐	☐

WEEK OF:

THURSDAY	FRIDAY	SATURDAY	SUNDAY

TO DO LIST

- ☐
- ☐
- ☐
- ☐
- ☐
- ☐
- ☐
- ☐

TASK LIST

- ☐
- ☐
- ☐
- ☐
- ☐
- ☐
- ☐
- ☐

WEEKLY NOTES

Order Tracker

DATE	CUSTOMER NAME	PRODUCT & ORDER AMOUNT	FOLLOW-UP

Downline Goal Progress

NAME   **GOAL**

UPDATE	DATE:	UPDATE	DATE:

NAME   **GOAL**

UPDATE	DATE:	UPDATE	DATE:

NAME   **GOAL**

UPDATE	DATE:	UPDATE	DATE:

Power Hour

DATE: _____

ADD NEW FRIENDS

_____
_____
_____
_____
_____

START NEW CONVERSATIONS

_____
_____
_____
_____
_____

RESPOND TO COMMENTS, MESSAGES, & EMAILS

_____
_____
_____
_____

SCHEDULE SOCIAL MEDIA POSTS

_____
_____
_____
_____

FOLLOW-UPS

_____

GOALS:

TASK LIST:

Power Hour

DATE: _____

ADD NEW FRIENDS

START NEW CONVERSATIONS

RESPOND TO COMMENTS, MESSAGES, & EMAILS

SCHEDULE SOCIAL MEDIA POSTS

FOLLOW-UPS

GOALS:

TASK LIST:

My Weekly Planner

TOP GOALS	MONDAY	TUESDAY	WEDNESDAY
☐			
☐			
☐			
☐			
☐			
☐			

TO DO:

- ☐
- ☐
- ☐
- ☐
- ☐
- ☐
- ☐
- ☐
- ☐
- ☐

BILLS TO PAY

	$
	$
	$
	$
	$

APPOINTMENTS//CALLS

HABIT TRACKER

	M	T	W	T	F	S	S
	☐	☐	☐	☐	☐	☐	☐
	☐	☐	☐	☐	☐	☐	☐
	☐	☐	☐	☐	☐	☐	☐
	☐	☐	☐	☐	☐	☐	☐
	☐	☐	☐	☐	☐	☐	☐
	☐	☐	☐	☐	☐	☐	☐

WEEK OF:

THURSDAY	FRIDAY	SATURDAY	SUNDAY

TO DO LIST

☐
☐
☐
☐
☐
☐
☐
☐

TASK LIST

☐
☐
☐
☐
☐
☐
☐
☐

WEEKLY NOTES

Order Tracker

WEEK OF:

DATE	CUSTOMER NAME	PRODUCT & ORDER AMOUNT	FOLLOW-UP

Downline Goal Progress

NAME	GOAL

UPDATE	DATE:	UPDATE	DATE:

NAME	GOAL

UPDATE	DATE:	UPDATE	DATE:

NAME	GOAL

UPDATE	DATE:	UPDATE	DATE:

Power Hour

DATE: _____

GOALS:

ADD NEW FRIENDS

_____
_____
_____
_____

START NEW CONVERSATIONS

_____
_____
_____
_____

RESPOND TO COMMENTS, MESSAGES, & EMAILS

_____
_____
_____
_____

SCHEDULE SOCIAL MEDIA POSTS

_____
_____
_____
_____

TASK LIST:

FOLLOW-UPS

_____
_____

Power Hour

DATE:

ADD NEW FRIENDS

START NEW CONVERSATIONS

RESPOND TO COMMENTS, MESSAGES, & EMAILS

SCHEDULE SOCIAL MEDIA POSTS

FOLLOW-UPS

GOALS:

TASK LIST:

My Weekly Planner

TOP GOALS	MONDAY	TUESDAY	WEDNESDAY
☐			
☐			
☐			
☐			
☐			
☐			

TO DO:

☐
☐
☐
☐
☐
☐
☐
☐
☐
☐

BILLS TO PAY

	$
_____	$
_____	$
_____	$
_____	$

APPOINTMENTS//CALLS

HABIT TRACKER	M	T	W	T	F	S	S
	☐	☐	☐	☐	☐	☐	☐
	☐	☐	☐	☐	☐	☐	☐
	☐	☐	☐	☐	☐	☐	☐
	☐	☐	☐	☐	☐	☐	☐
	☐	☐	☐	☐	☐	☐	☐
	☐	☐	☐	☐	☐	☐	☐

WEEK OF:

THURSDAY	FRIDAY	SATURDAY	SUNDAY

TO DO LIST

_____	☐
_____	☐
_____	☐
_____	☐
_____	☐
_____	☐
_____	☐
_____	☐

TASK LIST

☐
☐
☐
☐
☐
☐
☐
☐

WEEKLY NOTES

Order Tracker

WEEK OF:

DATE	CUSTOMER NAME	PRODUCT & ORDER AMOUNT	FOLLOW-UP

Downline Goal Progress

NAME **GOAL**

UPDATE DATE: **UPDATE** DATE:

NAME **GOAL**

UPDATE DATE: **UPDATE** DATE:

NAME **GOAL**

UPDATE DATE: **UPDATE** DATE:

Power Hour

DATE: _____

ADD NEW FRIENDS

START NEW CONVERSATIONS

RESPOND TO COMMENTS, MESSAGES, & EMAILS

SCHEDULE SOCIAL MEDIA POSTS

FOLLOW-UPS

GOALS:

TASK LIST:

Power Hour

DATE:

ADD NEW FRIENDS

START NEW CONVERSATIONS

RESPOND TO COMMENTS, MESSAGES, & EMAILS

SCHEDULE SOCIAL MEDIA POSTS

FOLLOW-UPS

GOALS:

TASK LIST:

My Weekly Planner

TOP GOALS	MONDAY	TUESDAY	WEDNESDAY
☐			
☐			
☐			
☐			
☐			
☐			

TO DO:

☐
☐
☐
☐
☐
☐
☐
☐
☐
☐

BILLS TO PAY

	$
	$
	$
	$
	$

APPOINTMENTS//CALLS

HABIT TRACKER

	M	T	W	T	F	S	S
	☐	☐	☐	☐	☐	☐	☐
	☐	☐	☐	☐	☐	☐	☐
	☐	☐	☐	☐	☐	☐	☐
	☐	☐	☐	☐	☐	☐	☐
	☐	☐	☐	☐	☐	☐	☐
	☐	☐	☐	☐	☐	☐	☐

WEEK OF:

THURSDAY	FRIDAY	SATURDAY	SUNDAY

TO DO LIST

- [ ] _____
- [ ] _____
- [ ] _____
- [ ] _____
- [ ] _____
- [ ] _____
- [ ] _____
- [ ] _____

TASK LIST

- [ ]
- [ ]
- [ ]
- [ ]
- [ ]
- [ ]
- [ ]
- [ ]

WEEKLY NOTES

_____
_____
_____
_____
_____
_____
_____

Order Tracker

DATE	CUSTOMER NAME	PRODUCT & ORDER AMOUNT	FOLLOW-UP

Downline Goal Progress

NAME	GOAL

UPDATE	DATE:	UPDATE	DATE:

NAME	GOAL

UPDATE	DATE:	UPDATE	DATE:

NAME	GOAL

UPDATE	DATE:	UPDATE	DATE:

Power Hour

DATE: _____

ADD NEW FRIENDS

_____
_____
_____
_____
_____

START NEW CONVERSATIONS

_____
_____
_____
_____
_____

RESPOND TO COMMENTS, MESSAGES, & EMAILS

_____
_____
_____
_____
_____

SCHEDULE SOCIAL MEDIA POSTS

_____
_____
_____
_____
_____

FOLLOW-UPS

_____
_____

GOALS:

TASK LIST:

Power Hour

DATE: _____

ADD NEW FRIENDS

_____
_____
_____
_____

START NEW CONVERSATIONS

_____
_____
_____
_____

RESPOND TO COMMENTS, MESSAGES, & EMAILS

_____
_____
_____
_____

SCHEDULE SOCIAL MEDIA POSTS

_____
_____
_____
_____

FOLLOW-UPS

_____

GOALS:

TASK LIST:

My Weekly Planner

TOP GOALS	MONDAY	TUESDAY	WEDNESDAY
☐			
☐			
☐			
☐			
☐			
☐			

TO DO:

☐
☐
☐
☐
☐
☐
☐
☐
☐
☐

BILLS TO PAY

_____ $
_____ $
_____ $
_____ $
_____ $

APPOINTMENTS//CALLS

HABIT TRACKER

HABIT TRACKER	M	T	W	T	F	S	S
	☐	☐	☐	☐	☐	☐	☐
	☐	☐	☐	☐	☐	☐	☐
	☐	☐	☐	☐	☐	☐	☐
	☐	☐	☐	☐	☐	☐	☐
	☐	☐	☐	☐	☐	☐	☐
	☐	☐	☐	☐	☐	☐	☐

WEEK OF:

THURSDAY	FRIDAY	SATURDAY	SUNDAY

TO DO LIST

- [ ] _____
- [ ] _____
- [ ] _____
- [ ] _____
- [ ] _____
- [ ] _____
- [ ] _____
- [ ] _____

TASK LIST

- [ ]
- [ ]
- [ ]
- [ ]
- [ ]
- [ ]
- [ ]
- [ ]

WEEKLY NOTES

_____
_____
_____
_____
_____
_____
_____

Order Tracker

DATE	CUSTOMER NAME	PRODUCT & ORDER AMOUNT	FOLLOW-UP

Downline Goal Progress

NAME   **GOAL**

U P D A T E   DATE: **U P D A T E**   DATE:

NAME   **GOAL**

U P D A T E   DATE: **U P D A T E**   DATE:

NAME   **GOAL**

U P D A T E   DATE: **U P D A T E**   DATE:

Power Hour

DATE:

ADD NEW FRIENDS

START NEW CONVERSATIONS

RESPOND TO COMMENTS, MESSAGES, & EMAILS

SCHEDULE SOCIAL MEDIA POSTS

FOLLOW-UPS

GOALS:

TASK LIST:

Power Hour

DATE:

ADD NEW FRIENDS

START NEW CONVERSATIONS

RESPOND TO COMMENTS, MESSAGES, & EMAILS

SCHEDULE SOCIAL MEDIA POSTS

FOLLOW-UPS

GOALS:

TASK LIST:

My Weekly Planner

TOP GOALS	MONDAY	TUESDAY	WEDNESDAY
☐			
☐			
☐			
☐			
☐			
☐			

TO DO:

- ☐
- ☐
- ☐
- ☐
- ☐
- ☐
- ☐
- ☐
- ☐
- ☐

BILLS TO PAY

_____	$
_____	$
_____	$
_____	$
_____	$

APPOINTMENTS//CALLS

HABIT TRACKER

HABIT TRACKER	M	T	W	T	F	S	S
	☐	☐	☐	☐	☐	☐	☐
	☐	☐	☐	☐	☐	☐	☐
	☐	☐	☐	☐	☐	☐	☐
	☐	☐	☐	☐	☐	☐	☐
	☐	☐	☐	☐	☐	☐	☐
	☐	☐	☐	☐	☐	☐	☐

WEEK OF:

THURSDAY	FRIDAY	SATURDAY	SUNDAY

TO DO LIST

- _____ ☐
- _____ ☐
- _____ ☐
- _____ ☐
- _____ ☐
- _____ ☐
- _____ ☐
- _____ ☐

TASK LIST

- ☐
- ☐
- ☐
- ☐
- ☐
- ☐
- ☐
- ☐

WEEKLY NOTES

Order Tracker

WEEK OF:

DATE	CUSTOMER NAME	PRODUCT & ORDER AMOUNT	FOLLOW-UP

Downline Goal Progress

NAME   GOAL

UPDATE   DATE: UPDATE   DATE:

NAME   GOAL

UPDATE   DATE: UPDATE   DATE:

NAME   GOAL

UPDATE   DATE: UPDATE   DATE:

Power Hour

DATE: _____

ADD NEW FRIENDS

START NEW CONVERSATIONS

RESPOND TO COMMENTS, MESSAGES, & EMAILS

SCHEDULE SOCIAL MEDIA POSTS

FOLLOW-UPS

GOALS:

TASK LIST:

Power Hour

DATE: _____

ADD NEW FRIENDS

START NEW CONVERSATIONS

RESPOND TO COMMENTS, MESSAGES, & EMAILS

SCHEDULE SOCIAL MEDIA POSTS

FOLLOW-UPS

GOALS:

TASK LIST:

My Weekly Planner

TOP GOALS	MONDAY	TUESDAY	WEDNESDAY
☐			
☐			
☐			
☐			
☐			
☐			

TO DO:

☐
☐
☐
☐
☐
☐
☐
☐
☐
☐

BILLS TO PAY

	$
	$
	$
	$
	$

APPOINTMENTS//CALLS

HABIT TRACKER

	M	T	W	T	F	S	S
	☐	☐	☐	☐	☐	☐	☐
	☐	☐	☐	☐	☐	☐	☐
	☐	☐	☐	☐	☐	☐	☐
	☐	☐	☐	☐	☐	☐	☐
	☐	☐	☐	☐	☐	☐	☐
	☐	☐	☐	☐	☐	☐	☐

WEEK OF:

THURSDAY	FRIDAY	SATURDAY	SUNDAY

TO DO LIST

- _____ ☐
- _____ ☐
- _____ ☐
- _____ ☐
- _____ ☐
- _____ ☐
- _____ ☐
- _____ ☐

TASK LIST

- ☐
- ☐
- ☐
- ☐
- ☐
- ☐
- ☐
- ☐

WEEKLY NOTES

_____

_____

_____

_____

_____

_____

_____

Order Tracker

WEEK OF:

DATE	CUSTOMER NAME	PRODUCT & ORDER AMOUNT	FOLLOW-UP

Downline Goal Progress

NAME   GOAL

UPDATE   DATE: UPDATE   DATE:

NAME   GOAL

UPDATE   DATE: UPDATE   DATE:

NAME   GOAL

UPDATE   DATE: UPDATE   DATE:

Power Hour

DATE: _____

ADD NEW FRIENDS

_____

_____

_____

_____

START NEW CONVERSATIONS

_____

_____

_____

_____

RESPOND TO COMMENTS, MESSAGES, & EMAILS

_____

_____

_____

_____

SCHEDULE SOCIAL MEDIA POSTS

_____

_____

_____

_____

FOLLOW-UPS

_____

_____

GOALS:

TASK LIST:

Power Hour

DATE: _____

ADD NEW FRIENDS

START NEW CONVERSATIONS

RESPOND TO COMMENTS, MESSAGES, & EMAILS

SCHEDULE SOCIAL MEDIA POSTS

FOLLOW-UPS

GOALS:

TASK LIST:

My Weekly Planner

TOP GOALS	MONDAY	TUESDAY	WEDNESDAY
☐			
☐			
☐			
☐			
☐			
☐			

TO DO:

☐

☐

☐

☐

☐

☐

☐

☐

☐

☐

BILLS TO PAY

_____ $ _____

_____ $ _____

_____ $ _____

_____ $ _____

_____ $ _____

APPOINTMENTS//CALLS

HABIT TRACKER	M	T	W	T	F	S	S
	☐	☐	☐	☐	☐	☐	☐
	☐	☐	☐	☐	☐	☐	☐
	☐	☐	☐	☐	☐	☐	☐
	☐	☐	☐	☐	☐	☐	☐
	☐	☐	☐	☐	☐	☐	☐
	☐	☐	☐	☐	☐	☐	☐

WEEK OF:

THURSDAY	FRIDAY	SATURDAY	SUNDAY

TO DO LIST

- ☐
- ☐
- ☐
- ☐
- ☐
- ☐
- ☐
- ☐

TASK LIST

- ☐
- ☐
- ☐
- ☐
- ☐
- ☐
- ☐
- ☐

WEEKLY NOTES

Order Tracker

WEEK OF:

DATE	CUSTOMER NAME	PRODUCT & ORDER AMOUNT	FOLLOW-UP

Downline Goal Progress

NAME   **GOAL**

U P D A T E   DATE:

U P D A T E   DATE:

NAME   **GOAL**

U P D A T E   DATE:

U P D A T E   DATE:

NAME   **GOAL**

U P D A T E   DATE:

U P D A T E   DATE:

Power Hour

DATE: _____

ADD NEW FRIENDS

START NEW CONVERSATIONS

RESPOND TO COMMENTS, MESSAGES, & EMAILS

SCHEDULE SOCIAL MEDIA POSTS

FOLLOW-UPS

GOALS:

TASK LIST:

Power Hour

DATE: _____

ADD NEW FRIENDS

START NEW CONVERSATIONS

RESPOND TO COMMENTS, MESSAGES, & EMAILS

SCHEDULE SOCIAL MEDIA POSTS

FOLLOW-UPS

GOALS:

TASK LIST:

My Weekly Planner

TOP GOALS	MONDAY	TUESDAY	WEDNESDAY
☐			
☐			
☐			
☐			
☐			
☐			

TO DO:

- ☐
- ☐
- ☐
- ☐
- ☐
- ☐
- ☐
- ☐
- ☐
- ☐

BILLS TO PAY

_____	$
_____	$
_____	$
_____	$
_____	$

APPOINTMENTS//CALLS

HABIT TRACKER

	M	T	W	T	F	S	S
	☐	☐	☐	☐	☐	☐	☐
	☐	☐	☐	☐	☐	☐	☐
	☐	☐	☐	☐	☐	☐	☐
	☐	☐	☐	☐	☐	☐	☐
	☐	☐	☐	☐	☐	☐	☐
	☐	☐	☐	☐	☐	☐	☐

WEEK OF:

THURSDAY	FRIDAY	SATURDAY	SUNDAY

TO DO LIST

- ☐
- ☐
- ☐
- ☐
- ☐
- ☐
- ☐
- ☐

TASK LIST

- ☐
- ☐
- ☐
- ☐
- ☐
- ☐
- ☐
- ☐

WEEKLY NOTES

Order Tracker

DATE	CUSTOMER NAME	PRODUCT & ORDER AMOUNT	FOLLOW-UP

Downline Goal Progress

NAME

GOAL

UPDATE   DATE:

UPDATE   DATE:

NAME

GOAL

UPDATE   DATE:

UPDATE   DATE:

NAME

GOAL

UPDATE   DATE:

UPDATE   DATE:

Power Hour

DATE:

GOALS:

ADD NEW FRIENDS

START NEW CONVERSATIONS

RESPOND TO COMMENTS, MESSAGES, & EMAILS

TASK LIST:

SCHEDULE SOCIAL MEDIA POSTS

FOLLOW-UPS

Power Hour

DATE: _____

ADD NEW FRIENDS

START NEW CONVERSATIONS

RESPOND TO COMMENTS, MESSAGES, & EMAILS

SCHEDULE SOCIAL MEDIA POSTS

FOLLOW-UPS

GOALS:

TASK LIST:

My Weekly Planner

TOP GOALS	MONDAY	TUESDAY	WEDNESDAY
☐			
☐			
☐			
☐			
☐			
☐			

TO DO:

- ☐
- ☐
- ☐
- ☐
- ☐
- ☐
- ☐
- ☐
- ☐
- ☐

BILLS TO PAY

_____ $_____

_____ $_____

_____ $_____

_____ $_____

_____ $_____

APPOINTMENTS//CALLS

HABIT TRACKER

	M	T	W	T	F	S	S
	☐	☐	☐	☐	☐	☐	☐
	☐	☐	☐	☐	☐	☐	☐
	☐	☐	☐	☐	☐	☐	☐
	☐	☐	☐	☐	☐	☐	☐
	☐	☐	☐	☐	☐	☐	☐
	☐	☐	☐	☐	☐	☐	☐

WEEK OF:

THURSDAY	FRIDAY	SATURDAY	SUNDAY

TO DO LIST

- [ ] _____
- [ ] _____
- [ ] _____
- [ ] _____
- [ ] _____
- [ ] _____
- [ ] _____
- [ ] _____

TASK LIST

- [ ]
- [ ]
- [ ]
- [ ]
- [ ]
- [ ]
- [ ]
- [ ]

WEEKLY NOTES

Order Tracker

WEEK OF:

DATE	CUSTOMER NAME	PRODUCT & ORDER AMOUNT	FOLLOW-UP

Downline Goal Progress

NAME **GOAL**

U P D A T E DATE:

U P D A T E DATE:

NAME **GOAL**

U P D A T E DATE:

U P D A T E DATE:

NAME **GOAL**

U P D A T E DATE:

U P D A T E DATE:

Power Hour

DATE:

ADD NEW FRIENDS

START NEW CONVERSATIONS

RESPOND TO COMMENTS, MESSAGES, & EMAILS

SCHEDULE SOCIAL MEDIA POSTS

FOLLOW-UPS

GOALS:

TASK LIST:

Power Hour

DATE:

ADD NEW FRIENDS

START NEW CONVERSATIONS

RESPOND TO COMMENTS, MESSAGES, & EMAILS

SCHEDULE SOCIAL MEDIA POSTS

FOLLOW-UPS

GOALS:

TASK LIST:

My Weekly Planner

TOP GOALS	MONDAY	TUESDAY	WEDNESDAY
☐			
☐			
☐			
☐			
☐			
☐			

TO DO:

- ☐
- ☐
- ☐
- ☐
- ☐
- ☐
- ☐
- ☐
- ☐
- ☐

BILLS TO PAY

	$
	$
	$
	$
	$

APPOINTMENTS//CALLS

HABIT TRACKER

	M	T	W	T	F	S	S
	☐	☐	☐	☐	☐	☐	☐
	☐	☐	☐	☐	☐	☐	☐
	☐	☐	☐	☐	☐	☐	☐
	☐	☐	☐	☐	☐	☐	☐
	☐	☐	☐	☐	☐	☐	☐
	☐	☐	☐	☐	☐	☐	☐

THURSDAY	FRIDAY	SATURDAY	SUNDAY

TO DO LIST

- _____ ☐
- _____ ☐
- _____ ☐
- _____ ☐
- _____ ☐
- _____ ☐
- _____ ☐
- _____ ☐

TASK LIST

- ☐
- ☐
- ☐
- ☐
- ☐
- ☐
- ☐
- ☐

WEEKLY NOTES

Order Tracker

WEEK OF:

DATE	CUSTOMER NAME	PRODUCT & ORDER AMOUNT	FOLLOW-UP

Downline Goal Progress

NAME   GOAL

UPDATE   DATE:

UPDATE   DATE:

NAME   GOAL

UPDATE   DATE:

UPDATE   DATE:

NAME   GOAL

UPDATE   DATE:

UPDATE   DATE:

Power Hour

DATE: _____

GOALS:

ADD NEW FRIENDS

START NEW CONVERSATIONS

RESPOND TO COMMENTS, MESSAGES, & EMAILS

SCHEDULE SOCIAL MEDIA POSTS

FOLLOW-UPS

TASK LIST:

Power Hour

DATE:

ADD NEW FRIENDS

START NEW CONVERSATIONS

RESPOND TO COMMENTS, MESSAGES, & EMAILS

SCHEDULE SOCIAL MEDIA POSTS

FOLLOW-UPS

GOALS:

TASK LIST:

My Weekly Planner

TOP GOALS	MONDAY	TUESDAY	WEDNESDAY
☐			
☐			
☐			
☐			
☐			
☐			

TO DO:

☐

☐

☐

☐

☐

☐

☐

☐

☐

☐

BILLS TO PAY

	$
	$
	$
	$
	$

APPOINTMENTS//CALLS

HABIT TRACKER

HABIT TRACKER	M	T	W	T	F	S	S
	☐	☐	☐	☐	☐	☐	☐
	☐	☐	☐	☐	☐	☐	☐
	☐	☐	☐	☐	☐	☐	☐
	☐	☐	☐	☐	☐	☐	☐
	☐	☐	☐	☐	☐	☐	☐
	☐	☐	☐	☐	☐	☐	☐

WEEK OF:

THURSDAY	FRIDAY	SATURDAY	SUNDAY

TO DO LIST

- _____ ☐
- _____ ☐
- _____ ☐
- _____ ☐
- _____ ☐
- _____ ☐
- _____ ☐
- _____ ☐

TASK LIST

- ☐
- ☐
- ☐
- ☐
- ☐
- ☐
- ☐
- ☐

WEEKLY NOTES

Order Tracker

WEEK OF:

DATE	CUSTOMER NAME	PRODUCT & ORDER AMOUNT	FOLLOW-UP

Downline Goal Progress

NAME   GOAL

UPDATE   DATE:

UPDATE   DATE:

NAME   GOAL

UPDATE   DATE:

UPDATE   DATE:

NAME   GOAL

UPDATE   DATE:

UPDATE   DATE:

Power Hour

DATE: _____

ADD NEW FRIENDS

START NEW CONVERSATIONS

RESPOND TO COMMENTS, MESSAGES, & EMAILS

SCHEDULE SOCIAL MEDIA POSTS

FOLLOW-UPS

GOALS:

TASK LIST:

Power Hour

DATE: _____

ADD NEW FRIENDS

START NEW CONVERSATIONS

RESPOND TO COMMENTS, MESSAGES, & EMAILS

SCHEDULE SOCIAL MEDIA POSTS

FOLLOW-UPS

GOALS:

TASK LIST:

My Weekly Planner

TOP GOALS	MONDAY	TUESDAY	WEDNESDAY
☐			
☐			
☐			
☐			
☐			
☐			

TO DO:

☐
☐
☐
☐
☐
☐
☐
☐
☐
☐

BILLS TO PAY

$
$
$
$
$

APPOINTMENTS//CALLS

HABIT TRACKER	M	T	W	T	F	S	S
	☐	☐	☐	☐	☐	☐	☐
	☐	☐	☐	☐	☐	☐	☐
	☐	☐	☐	☐	☐	☐	☐
	☐	☐	☐	☐	☐	☐	☐
	☐	☐	☐	☐	☐	☐	☐
	☐	☐	☐	☐	☐	☐	☐

WEEK OF:

THURSDAY	FRIDAY	SATURDAY	SUNDAY

TO DO LIST

- [ ]
- [ ]
- [ ]
- [ ]
- [ ]
- [ ]
- [ ]
- [ ]

TASK LIST

- [ ]
- [ ]
- [ ]
- [ ]
- [ ]
- [ ]
- [ ]
- [ ]

WEEKLY NOTES

Order Tracker

DATE	CUSTOMER NAME	PRODUCT & ORDER AMOUNT	FOLLOW-UP

Downline Goal Progress

NAME   GOAL

UPDATE   DATE: UPDATE   DATE:

NAME   GOAL

UPDATE   DATE: UPDATE   DATE:

NAME   GOAL

UPDATE   DATE: UPDATE   DATE:

Power Hour

DATE: _____

ADD NEW FRIENDS

_____
_____
_____
_____

START NEW CONVERSATIONS

_____
_____
_____
_____

RESPOND TO COMMENTS, MESSAGES, & EMAILS

_____
_____
_____
_____

SCHEDULE SOCIAL MEDIA POSTS

_____
_____
_____
_____

FOLLOW-UPS

_____
_____

GOALS:

TASK LIST:

Power Hour

DATE: _____

ADD NEW FRIENDS

START NEW CONVERSATIONS

RESPOND TO COMMENTS, MESSAGES, & EMAILS

SCHEDULE SOCIAL MEDIA POSTS

FOLLOW-UPS

GOALS:

TASK LIST:

My Weekly Planner

TOP GOALS	MONDAY	TUESDAY	WEDNESDAY
☐			
☐			
☐			
☐			
☐			
☐			

TO DO:

☐
☐
☐
☐
☐
☐
☐
☐
☐
☐

BILLS TO PAY

	$
	$
	$
	$
	$

APPOINTMENTS//CALLS

HABIT TRACKER

	M	T	W	T	F	S	S
	☐	☐	☐	☐	☐	☐	☐
	☐	☐	☐	☐	☐	☐	☐
	☐	☐	☐	☐	☐	☐	☐
	☐	☐	☐	☐	☐	☐	☐
	☐	☐	☐	☐	☐	☐	☐
	☐	☐	☐	☐	☐	☐	☐

WEEK OF:

THURSDAY	FRIDAY	SATURDAY	SUNDAY

TO DO LIST

- ☐
- ☐
- ☐
- ☐
- ☐
- ☐
- ☐
- ☐

TASK LIST

- ☐
- ☐
- ☐
- ☐
- ☐
- ☐
- ☐
- ☐

WEEKLY NOTES

Order Tracker

WEEK OF:

DATE	CUSTOMER NAME	PRODUCT & ORDER AMOUNT	FOLLOW-UP

Downline Goal Progress

NAME	GOAL

UPDATE	DATE:	UPDATE	DATE:

NAME	GOAL

UPDATE	DATE:	UPDATE	DATE:

NAME	GOAL

UPDATE	DATE:	UPDATE	DATE:

Power Hour

DATE: _____

ADD NEW FRIENDS

_____
_____
_____
_____

START NEW CONVERSATIONS

_____
_____
_____
_____

RESPOND TO COMMENTS, MESSAGES, & EMAILS

_____
_____
_____
_____

SCHEDULE SOCIAL MEDIA POSTS

_____
_____
_____
_____

FOLLOW-UPS

_____   _____
_____   _____

GOALS:

TASK LIST:

Power Hour

DATE: _____

ADD NEW FRIENDS

START NEW CONVERSATIONS

RESPOND TO COMMENTS, MESSAGES, & EMAILS

SCHEDULE SOCIAL MEDIA POSTS

FOLLOW-UPS

GOALS:

TASK LIST:

My Weekly Planner

TOP GOALS	MONDAY	TUESDAY	WEDNESDAY
☐			
☐			
☐			
☐			
☐			
☐			

TO DO:

☐
☐
☐
☐
☐
☐
☐
☐
☐
☐

BILLS TO PAY

	$
	$
	$
	$
	$

APPOINTMENTS//CALLS

HABIT TRACKER

	M	T	W	T	F	S	S
	☐	☐	☐	☐	☐	☐	☐
	☐	☐	☐	☐	☐	☐	☐
	☐	☐	☐	☐	☐	☐	☐
	☐	☐	☐	☐	☐	☐	☐
	☐	☐	☐	☐	☐	☐	☐
	☐	☐	☐	☐	☐	☐	☐

WEEK OF:

THURSDAY	FRIDAY	SATURDAY	SUNDAY

TO DO LIST

- ☐
- ☐
- ☐
- ☐
- ☐
- ☐
- ☐
- ☐

TASK LIST

- ☐
- ☐
- ☐
- ☐
- ☐
- ☐
- ☐
- ☐

WEEKLY NOTES

Order Tracker

WEEK OF:

DATE	CUSTOMER NAME	PRODUCT & ORDER AMOUNT	FOLLOW-UP

Downline Goal Progress

NAME	GOAL

UPDATE	DATE:	UPDATE	DATE:

NAME	GOAL

UPDATE	DATE:	UPDATE	DATE:

NAME	GOAL

UPDATE	DATE:	UPDATE	DATE:

Power Hour

DATE:

ADD NEW FRIENDS

START NEW CONVERSATIONS

RESPOND TO COMMENTS, MESSAGES, & EMAILS

SCHEDULE SOCIAL MEDIA POSTS

FOLLOW-UPS

GOALS:

TASK LIST:

Power Hour

DATE: _____

ADD NEW FRIENDS

START NEW CONVERSATIONS

RESPOND TO COMMENTS, MESSAGES, & EMAILS

SCHEDULE SOCIAL MEDIA POSTS

FOLLOW-UPS

GOALS:

TASK LIST:

My Weekly Planner

TOP GOALS	MONDAY	TUESDAY	WEDNESDAY
☐			
☐			
☐			
☐			
☐			
☐			

TO DO:

☐
☐
☐
☐
☐
☐
☐
☐
☐
☐

BILLS TO PAY

	$
	$
	$
	$
	$

APPOINTMENTS//CALLS

HABIT TRACKER

	M	T	W	T	F	S	S
	☐	☐	☐	☐	☐	☐	☐
	☐	☐	☐	☐	☐	☐	☐
	☐	☐	☐	☐	☐	☐	☐
	☐	☐	☐	☐	☐	☐	☐
	☐	☐	☐	☐	☐	☐	☐
	☐	☐	☐	☐	☐	☐	☐

WEEK OF:

THURSDAY	FRIDAY	SATURDAY	SUNDAY

TO DO LIST

_____ ☐

_____ ☐

_____ ☐

_____ ☐

_____ ☐

_____ ☐

_____ ☐

_____ ☐

TASK LIST

☐

☐

☐

☐

☐

☐

☐

☐

WEEKLY NOTES

_____

_____

_____

_____

_____

_____

_____

Order Tracker

DATE	CUSTOMER NAME	PRODUCT & ORDER AMOUNT	FOLLOW-UP

Downline Goal Progress

NAME

GOAL

UPDATE   DATE:

UPDATE   DATE:

NAME

GOAL

UPDATE   DATE:

UPDATE   DATE:

NAME

GOAL

UPDATE   DATE:

UPDATE   DATE:

Power Hour

DATE:

ADD NEW FRIENDS

START NEW CONVERSATIONS

RESPOND TO COMMENTS, MESSAGES, & EMAILS

SCHEDULE SOCIAL MEDIA POSTS

FOLLOW-UPS

GOALS:

TASK LIST:

Power Hour

DATE: _____

ADD NEW FRIENDS

START NEW CONVERSATIONS

RESPOND TO COMMENTS, MESSAGES, & EMAILS

SCHEDULE SOCIAL MEDIA POSTS

FOLLOW-UPS

GOALS:

TASK LIST:

My Weekly Planner

TOP GOALS	MONDAY	TUESDAY	WEDNESDAY
☐			
☐			
☐			
☐			
☐			
☐			

TO DO:

☐
☐
☐
☐
☐
☐
☐
☐
☐
☐

BILLS TO PAY

	$
	$
	$
	$
	$

APPOINTMENTS//CALLS

HABIT TRACKER

	M	T	W	T	F	S	S
	☐	☐	☐	☐	☐	☐	☐
	☐	☐	☐	☐	☐	☐	☐
	☐	☐	☐	☐	☐	☐	☐
	☐	☐	☐	☐	☐	☐	☐
	☐	☐	☐	☐	☐	☐	☐
	☐	☐	☐	☐	☐	☐	☐

WEEK OF:

THURSDAY	FRIDAY	SATURDAY	SUNDAY

TO DO LIST

_____ ☐
_____ ☐
_____ ☐
_____ ☐
_____ ☐
_____ ☐
_____ ☐
                   ☐

TASK LIST

☐
☐
☐
☐
☐
☐
☐
☐

WEEKLY NOTES

_____
_____
_____
_____
_____
_____
_____

Order Tracker

DATE	CUSTOMER NAME	PRODUCT & ORDER AMOUNT	FOLLOW-UP

Downline Goal Progress

NAME	GOAL

UPDATE	DATE:	UPDATE	DATE:

NAME	GOAL

UPDATE	DATE:	UPDATE	DATE:

NAME	GOAL

UPDATE	DATE:	UPDATE	DATE:

Power Hour

DATE: _____

ADD NEW FRIENDS

START NEW CONVERSATIONS

RESPOND TO COMMENTS, MESSAGES, & EMAILS

SCHEDULE SOCIAL MEDIA POSTS

FOLLOW-UPS

GOALS:

TASK LIST:

Power Hour

DATE: _____

ADD NEW FRIENDS

START NEW CONVERSATIONS

RESPOND TO COMMENTS, MESSAGES, & EMAILS

SCHEDULE SOCIAL MEDIA POSTS

FOLLOW-UPS

GOALS:

TASK LIST:

My Weekly Planner

TOP GOALS	MONDAY	TUESDAY	WEDNESDAY
☐			
☐			
☐			
☐			
☐			
☐			

TO DO:

☐
☐
☐
☐
☐
☐
☐
☐
☐
☐

BILLS TO PAY

	$
	$
	$
	$
	$

APPOINTMENTS//CALLS

HABIT TRACKER

	M	T	W	T	F	S	S
	☐	☐	☐	☐	☐	☐	☐
	☐	☐	☐	☐	☐	☐	☐
	☐	☐	☐	☐	☐	☐	☐
	☐	☐	☐	☐	☐	☐	☐
	☐	☐	☐	☐	☐	☐	☐
	☐	☐	☐	☐	☐	☐	☐

WEEK OF:

THURSDAY	FRIDAY	SATURDAY	SUNDAY

TO DO LIST

- ☐
- ☐
- ☐
- ☐
- ☐
- ☐
- ☐
- ☐

TASK LIST

- ☐
- ☐
- ☐
- ☐
- ☐
- ☐
- ☐
- ☐

WEEKLY NOTES

Order Tracker

WEEK OF:

DATE	CUSTOMER NAME	PRODUCT & ORDER AMOUNT	FOLLOW-UP

Downline Goal Progress

NAME | **GOAL**

UPDATE | DATE:

UPDATE | DATE:

NAME | **GOAL**

UPDATE | DATE:

UPDATE | DATE:

NAME | **GOAL**

UPDATE | DATE:

UPDATE | DATE:

Power Hour

DATE: _____

ADD NEW FRIENDS

_____
_____
_____
_____

START NEW CONVERSATIONS

_____
_____
_____
_____

RESPOND TO COMMENTS, MESSAGES, & EMAILS

_____
_____
_____

SCHEDULE SOCIAL MEDIA POSTS

_____
_____
_____

FOLLOW-UPS

_____

GOALS:

TASK LIST:

Power Hour

DATE:

ADD NEW FRIENDS

START NEW CONVERSATIONS

RESPOND TO COMMENTS, MESSAGES, & EMAILS

SCHEDULE SOCIAL MEDIA POSTS

FOLLOW-UPS

GOALS:

TASK LIST:

My Weekly Planner

TOP GOALS	MONDAY	TUESDAY	WEDNESDAY
☐			
☐			
☐			
☐			
☐			
☐			

TO DO:

☐
☐
☐
☐
☐
☐
☐
☐
☐
☐

BILLS TO PAY

	$
	$
	$
	$
	$

APPOINTMENTS//CALLS

HABIT TRACKER

HABIT TRACKER	M	T	W	T	F	S	S
	☐	☐	☐	☐	☐	☐	☐
	☐	☐	☐	☐	☐	☐	☐
	☐	☐	☐	☐	☐	☐	☐
	☐	☐	☐	☐	☐	☐	☐
	☐	☐	☐	☐	☐	☐	☐
	☐	☐	☐	☐	☐	☐	☐

WEEK OF:

THURSDAY	FRIDAY	SATURDAY	SUNDAY

TO DO LIST

- [ ]
- [ ]
- [ ]
- [ ]
- [ ]
- [ ]
- [ ]
- [ ]

TASK LIST

- [ ]
- [ ]
- [ ]
- [ ]
- [ ]
- [ ]
- [ ]
- [ ]

WEEKLY NOTES

Order Tracker

WEEK OF:

DATE	CUSTOMER NAME	PRODUCT & ORDER AMOUNT	FOLLOW-UP

Downline Goal Progress

NAME	GOAL

UPDATE	DATE:	UPDATE	DATE:

NAME	GOAL

UPDATE	DATE:	UPDATE	DATE:

NAME	GOAL

UPDATE	DATE:	UPDATE	DATE:

Power Hour

DATE: _____

ADD NEW FRIENDS

_____
_____
_____
_____
_____

START NEW CONVERSATIONS

_____
_____
_____
_____
_____

RESPOND TO COMMENTS, MESSAGES, & EMAILS

_____
_____
_____
_____
_____

SCHEDULE SOCIAL MEDIA POSTS

_____
_____
_____
_____
_____

FOLLOW-UPS

_____
_____

GOALS:

TASK LIST:

Power Hour

DATE: _____

ADD NEW FRIENDS

START NEW CONVERSATIONS

RESPOND TO COMMENTS, MESSAGES, & EMAILS

SCHEDULE SOCIAL MEDIA POSTS

FOLLOW-UPS

GOALS:

TASK LIST:

My Weekly Planner

TOP GOALS	MONDAY	TUESDAY	WEDNESDAY
☐			
☐			
☐			
☐			
☐			
☐			

TO DO:

☐
☐
☐
☐
☐
☐
☐
☐
☐
☐

BILLS TO PAY

	$
	$
	$
	$
	$

APPOINTMENTS//CALLS

HABIT TRACKER

	M	T	W	T	F	S	S
	☐	☐	☐	☐	☐	☐	☐
	☐	☐	☐	☐	☐	☐	☐
	☐	☐	☐	☐	☐	☐	☐
	☐	☐	☐	☐	☐	☐	☐
	☐	☐	☐	☐	☐	☐	☐
	☐	☐	☐	☐	☐	☐	☐

WEEK OF:

THURSDAY	FRIDAY	SATURDAY	SUNDAY

TO DO LIST

- ☐
- ☐
- ☐
- ☐
- ☐
- ☐
- ☐
- ☐

TASK LIST

- ☐
- ☐
- ☐
- ☐
- ☐
- ☐
- ☐
- ☐

WEEKLY NOTES

Order Tracker

WEEK OF:

DATE	CUSTOMER NAME	PRODUCT & ORDER AMOUNT	FOLLOW-UP

Downline Goal Progress

NAME	GOAL

UPDATE	DATE:	UPDATE	DATE:

NAME	GOAL

UPDATE	DATE:	UPDATE	DATE:

NAME	GOAL

UPDATE	DATE:	UPDATE	DATE:

Power Hour

DATE: ....

ADD NEW FRIENDS

START NEW CONVERSATIONS

RESPOND TO COMMENTS, MESSAGES, & EMAILS

SCHEDULE SOCIAL MEDIA POSTS

FOLLOW-UPS

GOALS:

TASK LIST:

Power Hour

DATE: _____

ADD NEW FRIENDS

START NEW CONVERSATIONS

RESPOND TO COMMENTS, MESSAGES, & EMAILS

SCHEDULE SOCIAL MEDIA POSTS

FOLLOW-UPS

GOALS:

TASK LIST:

My Weekly Planner

TOP GOALS	MONDAY	TUESDAY	WEDNESDAY
☐			
☐			
☐			
☐			
☐			
☐			

TO DO:

☐
☐
☐
☐
☐
☐
☐
☐
☐
☐

BILLS TO PAY

	$
	$
	$
	$
	$

APPOINTMENTS//CALLS

HABIT TRACKER

	M	T	W	T	F	S	S
	☐	☐	☐	☐	☐	☐	☐
	☐	☐	☐	☐	☐	☐	☐
	☐	☐	☐	☐	☐	☐	☐
	☐	☐	☐	☐	☐	☐	☐
	☐	☐	☐	☐	☐	☐	☐
	☐	☐	☐	☐	☐	☐	☐

WEEK OF:

THURSDAY	FRIDAY	SATURDAY	SUNDAY

TO DO LIST

- ☐ _____
- ☐ _____
- ☐ _____
- ☐ _____
- ☐ _____
- ☐ _____
- ☐ _____
- ☐ _____

TASK LIST

- ☐
- ☐
- ☐
- ☐
- ☐
- ☐
- ☐
- ☐

WEEKLY NOTES

_____
_____
_____
_____
_____
_____
_____

Order Tracker

WEEK OF:

DATE	CUSTOMER NAME	PRODUCT & ORDER AMOUNT	FOLLOW-UP

Downline Goal Progress

NAME	GOAL

UPDATE	DATE:	UPDATE	DATE:

NAME	GOAL

UPDATE	DATE:	UPDATE	DATE:

NAME	GOAL

UPDATE	DATE:	UPDATE	DATE:

Power Hour

DATE: _____

GOALS:

ADD NEW FRIENDS

START NEW CONVERSATIONS

RESPOND TO COMMENTS, MESSAGES, & EMAILS

TASK LIST:

SCHEDULE SOCIAL MEDIA POSTS

FOLLOW-UPS

Power Hour

DATE:

ADD NEW FRIENDS

START NEW CONVERSATIONS

RESPOND TO COMMENTS, MESSAGES, & EMAILS

SCHEDULE SOCIAL MEDIA POSTS

FOLLOW-UPS

GOALS:

TASK LIST:

My Weekly Planner

TOP GOALS	MONDAY	TUESDAY	WEDNESDAY
☐			
☐			
☐			
☐			
☐			
☐			

TO DO:

☐
☐
☐
☐
☐
☐
☐
☐
☐
☐

BILLS TO PAY

_____ $ _____
_____ $ _____
_____ $ _____
_____ $ _____
_____ $ _____

APPOINTMENTS//CALLS

HABIT TRACKER

	M	T	W	T	F	S	S
	☐	☐	☐	☐	☐	☐	☐
	☐	☐	☐	☐	☐	☐	☐
	☐	☐	☐	☐	☐	☐	☐
	☐	☐	☐	☐	☐	☐	☐
	☐	☐	☐	☐	☐	☐	☐
	☐	☐	☐	☐	☐	☐	☐

WEEK OF:

THURSDAY	FRIDAY	SATURDAY	SUNDAY

TO DO LIST

- ☐
- ☐
- ☐
- ☐
- ☐
- ☐
- ☐
- ☐

TASK LIST

- ☐
- ☐
- ☐
- ☐
- ☐
- ☐
- ☐
- ☐

WEEKLY NOTES

Order Tracker

DATE	CUSTOMER NAME	PRODUCT & ORDER AMOUNT	FOLLOW-UP

Downline Goal Progress

NAME	GOAL

UPDATE	DATE:	UPDATE	DATE:

NAME	GOAL

UPDATE	DATE:	UPDATE	DATE:

NAME	GOAL

UPDATE	DATE:	UPDATE	DATE:

Power Hour

DATE:

ADD NEW FRIENDS

START NEW CONVERSATIONS

RESPOND TO COMMENTS, MESSAGES, & EMAILS

SCHEDULE SOCIAL MEDIA POSTS

FOLLOW-UPS

GOALS:

TASK LIST:

Power Hour

DATE: _____

ADD NEW FRIENDS

START NEW CONVERSATIONS

RESPOND TO COMMENTS, MESSAGES, & EMAILS

SCHEDULE SOCIAL MEDIA POSTS

FOLLOW-UPS

GOALS:

TASK LIST:

My Weekly Planner

TOP GOALS	MONDAY	TUESDAY	WEDNESDAY
☐			
☐			
☐			
☐			
☐			
☐			

TO DO:

- ☐
- ☐
- ☐
- ☐
- ☐
- ☐
- ☐
- ☐
- ☐
- ☐

BILLS TO PAY

	$
	$
	$
	$
	$

APPOINTMENTS//CALLS

HABIT TRACKER

	M	T	W	T	F	S	S
	☐	☐	☐	☐	☐	☐	☐
	☐	☐	☐	☐	☐	☐	☐
	☐	☐	☐	☐	☐	☐	☐
	☐	☐	☐	☐	☐	☐	☐
	☐	☐	☐	☐	☐	☐	☐
	☐	☐	☐	☐	☐	☐	☐

WEEK OF:

THURSDAY	FRIDAY	SATURDAY	SUNDAY

TO DO LIST

- [ ]
- [ ]
- [ ]
- [ ]
- [ ]
- [ ]
- [ ]
- [ ]

TASK LIST

- [ ]
- [ ]
- [ ]
- [ ]
- [ ]
- [ ]
- [ ]
- [ ]

WEEKLY NOTES

Order Tracker

WEEK OF:

DATE	CUSTOMER NAME	PRODUCT & ORDER AMOUNT	FOLLOW-UP

Downline Goal Progress

NAME	GOAL

UPDATE	DATE:	UPDATE	DATE:

NAME	GOAL

UPDATE	DATE:	UPDATE	DATE:

NAME	GOAL

UPDATE	DATE:	UPDATE	DATE:

Power Hour

DATE:

ADD NEW FRIENDS

START NEW CONVERSATIONS

RESPOND TO COMMENTS, MESSAGES, & EMAILS

SCHEDULE SOCIAL MEDIA POSTS

FOLLOW-UPS

GOALS:

TASK LIST:

Power Hour

DATE: _____

ADD NEW FRIENDS

START NEW CONVERSATIONS

RESPOND TO COMMENTS, MESSAGES, & EMAILS

SCHEDULE SOCIAL MEDIA POSTS

FOLLOW-UPS

GOALS:

TASK LIST:

My Weekly Planner

TOP GOALS	MONDAY	TUESDAY	WEDNESDAY
☐			
☐			
☐			
☐			
☐			
☐			

TO DO:

☐

☐

☐

☐

☐

☐

☐

☐

☐

☐

BILLS TO PAY

_____ $_____

_____ $_____

_____ $_____

_____ $_____

_____ $_____

APPOINTMENTS//CALLS

HABIT TRACKER

	M	T	W	T	F	S	S
	☐	☐	☐	☐	☐	☐	☐
	☐	☐	☐	☐	☐	☐	☐
	☐	☐	☐	☐	☐	☐	☐
	☐	☐	☐	☐	☐	☐	☐
	☐	☐	☐	☐	☐	☐	☐
	☐	☐	☐	☐	☐	☐	☐

WEEK OF:

THURSDAY	FRIDAY	SATURDAY	SUNDAY

TO DO LIST

- _____ ☐
- _____ ☐
- _____ ☐
- _____ ☐
- _____ ☐
- _____ ☐
- _____ ☐
- _____ ☐

TASK LIST

☐
☐
☐
☐
☐
☐
☐
☐

WEEKLY NOTES

_____
_____
_____
_____
_____
_____
_____

Order Tracker

WEEK OF:

DATE	CUSTOMER NAME	PRODUCT & ORDER AMOUNT	FOLLOW-UP

Downline Goal Progress

NAME   **GOAL**

UPDATE   DATE: **UPDATE**   DATE:

NAME   **GOAL**

UPDATE   DATE: **UPDATE**   DATE:

NAME   **GOAL**

UPDATE   DATE: **UPDATE**   DATE:

Power Hour

DATE: _____

ADD NEW FRIENDS

_____
_____
_____
_____

START NEW CONVERSATIONS

_____
_____
_____
_____

RESPOND TO COMMENTS, MESSAGES, & EMAILS

_____
_____
_____
_____

SCHEDULE SOCIAL MEDIA POSTS

_____
_____
_____
_____

FOLLOW-UPS

_____ _____

GOALS:

TASK LIST:

Power Hour

DATE:

ADD NEW FRIENDS

START NEW CONVERSATIONS

RESPOND TO COMMENTS, MESSAGES, & EMAILS

SCHEDULE SOCIAL MEDIA POSTS

FOLLOW-UPS

GOALS:

TASK LIST:

My Weekly Planner

TOP GOALS	MONDAY	TUESDAY	WEDNESDAY
☐			
☐			
☐			
☐			
☐			
☐			

TO DO:

☐
☐
☐
☐
☐
☐
☐
☐
☐
☐

BILLS TO PAY

	$
	$
	$
	$
	$

APPOINTMENTS//CALLS

HABIT TRACKER

	M	T	W	T	F	S	S
	☐	☐	☐	☐	☐	☐	☐
	☐	☐	☐	☐	☐	☐	☐
	☐	☐	☐	☐	☐	☐	☐
	☐	☐	☐	☐	☐	☐	☐
	☐	☐	☐	☐	☐	☐	☐
	☐	☐	☐	☐	☐	☐	☐

WEEK OF:

THURSDAY	FRIDAY	SATURDAY	SUNDAY

TO DO LIST

- ☐
- ☐
- ☐
- ☐
- ☐
- ☐
- ☐
- ☐

TASK LIST

- ☐
- ☐
- ☐
- ☐
- ☐
- ☐
- ☐
- ☐

WEEKLY NOTES

Order Tracker

WEEK OF:

DATE	CUSTOMER NAME	PRODUCT & ORDER AMOUNT	FOLLOW-UP

Downline Goal Progress

NAME	GOAL

UPDATE	DATE:	UPDATE	DATE:

NAME	GOAL

UPDATE	DATE:	UPDATE	DATE:

NAME	GOAL

UPDATE	DATE:	UPDATE	DATE:

Power Hour

DATE: _____

ADD NEW FRIENDS

START NEW CONVERSATIONS

RESPOND TO COMMENTS, MESSAGES, & EMAILS

SCHEDULE SOCIAL MEDIA POSTS

FOLLOW-UPS

GOALS:

TASK LIST:

Power Hour

DATE: _____

ADD NEW FRIENDS

_____
_____
_____
_____

START NEW CONVERSATIONS

_____
_____
_____
_____
_____

RESPOND TO COMMENTS, MESSAGES, & EMAILS

_____
_____
_____
_____
_____

SCHEDULE SOCIAL MEDIA POSTS

_____
_____
_____
_____

FOLLOW-UPS

_____   _____

GOALS:

TASK LIST:

My Weekly Planner

TOP GOALS	MONDAY	TUESDAY	WEDNESDAY
☐			
☐			
☐			
☐			
☐			
☐			

TO DO:

☐
☐
☐
☐
☐
☐
☐
☐
☐
☐

BILLS TO PAY

$
$
$
$
$

APPOINTMENTS//CALLS

HABIT TRACKER

	M	T	W	T	F	S	S
	☐	☐	☐	☐	☐	☐	☐
	☐	☐	☐	☐	☐	☐	☐
	☐	☐	☐	☐	☐	☐	☐
	☐	☐	☐	☐	☐	☐	☐
	☐	☐	☐	☐	☐	☐	☐
	☐	☐	☐	☐	☐	☐	☐

WEEK OF:

THURSDAY	FRIDAY	SATURDAY	SUNDAY

TO DO LIST

_____	☐
_____	☐
_____	☐
_____	☐
_____	☐
_____	☐
_____	☐
_____	☐

TASK LIST

☐
☐
☐
☐
☐
☐
☐
☐

WEEKLY NOTES

Order Tracker

DATE	CUSTOMER NAME	PRODUCT & ORDER AMOUNT	FOLLOW-UP

Downline Goal Progress

NAME	GOAL

UPDATE	DATE:

UPDATE	DATE:

NAME	GOAL

UPDATE	DATE:

UPDATE	DATE:

NAME	GOAL

UPDATE	DATE:

UPDATE	DATE:

Power Hour

DATE: _____

ADD NEW FRIENDS

_____
_____
_____
_____

START NEW CONVERSATIONS

_____
_____
_____
_____

RESPOND TO COMMENTS, MESSAGES, & EMAILS

_____
_____
_____
_____

SCHEDULE SOCIAL MEDIA POSTS

_____
_____
_____
_____

FOLLOW-UPS

_____

GOALS:

TASK LIST:

Power Hour

DATE: _____

ADD NEW FRIENDS

START NEW CONVERSATIONS

RESPOND TO COMMENTS, MESSAGES, & EMAILS

SCHEDULE SOCIAL MEDIA POSTS

FOLLOW-UPS

GOALS:

TASK LIST:

Made in the USA
Columbia, SC
11 March 2022

57548321R00087